THE SEVEN LAST WORDS OF Jesus

THE SEVEN
LAST WORDS
OF *Jesus*

Romanus Cessario, O.P.

MAGNIFICAT®
Paris / New York

Publisher: Pierre-Marie Dumont
Copy editor: Susan Barnes
Proofreader: Janet Chevrier
Art Direction: Elisabeth Hébert
Iconography: Isabelle Mascaras
Layout: Anaïs Acker
Production: Thierry Dubus
Concept and Design: MAGNIFICAT® (Romain Lizé, Marthe Rollier)

Artwork: *Painted Cross with Scenes from the Passion*, Master of Rosano, 12th century,
from the Abbey of Santa Maria Assunta di Rosano, Italy.
All pictures © Su concessione del Ministero per i Beni e le Attività Culturali – Opificio delle Pietre
Dure di Firenze, Italy, Archivio Fotografico.
ISBN: 978-0-9798086-4-7
First edition: February 2009
© MAGNIFICAT USA LLC
All rights reserved.

Printed in Canada

Aux deux Pierre,

Pierre-Marie Dumont et Peter John Cameron, O.P.,

qui, bâtissant sur la Pierre d'angle, construisent MAGNIFICAT.

THE SEVEN
LAST WORDS
OF
Jesus

Illustrations from *Painted Cross with Scenes from the Passion*
Master of Rosano, 12th century
Abbey of Santa Maria Assunta di Rosano, Italy.

Foreword

*O*ne hesitates to play the prophet. Nonetheless, I dare to forecast that the Reverend Romanus Cessario's splendid meditation on the seven last words of Our Lord and Savior will be a treasure-house of theology and spirituality for Catholics and non-Catholics alike for many, many years to come.

Father Cessario writes powerfully and lovingly about each of the seven statements uttered by the Son of God on Calvary's cross and finds in each of them a remarkable expression of the "divine order," the theme that underlies his entire composition.

The ease with which he cites Scripture, the Fathers and Doctors of the Church, and theologians of all eras never ceases to amaze. One immediately senses that we are being taught and inspired by a deeply committed follower of the Lord who loves and reveres all that the Church teaches and earnestly desires to share it with others.

In this volume, Father Cessario not only illuminates each of the Savior's seven last words; he also deftly draws into his analysis a number of timely and crucially important issues that one might not expect to be treated in these pages. Christian marriage, the Eucharist, vocations, chastity, and liturgy are but a few examples, all of which are woven into the total fabric of his work with clarity and skill. Like the "Scribe instructed in the Kingdom of heaven," he generously "brings forth from his storeroom things both new and old" (Mt 13:52).

In the name of the thousands who heard Father Cessario on Good Friday 2008 in Saint Patrick's Cathedral and the thousands more who will have an opportunity to read and meditate these pages, and in my own name as well, I express my admiration and heartfelt gratitude to this extraordinary theologian and preacher.

Edward Cardinal Egan
Archbishop of New York

November 24, 2008

Introduction

*I*t was now about noon and darkness came over the whole land until three in the afternoon because of an eclipse of the sun" (Lk 23: 44–45a). It is now noontime in Manhattan. Good Friday. The Christian world comes to a stop. Everywhere Christian believers halt their ordinary routines. They interrupt their work and their play. They leave behind their preoccupations. A symbolic darkness falls over the Christian people. This seclusion helps them to observe the most important three hours in the history of the world. These three hours. From about noon until three in the afternoon. Today. The day when Jesus dies… Although every liturgical season proclaims in some way the death of the Lord, Lent and Easter do so exceptionally. This past Lenten period allowed time for focused reflection on Christ's Passion and death. We deepened our devotion to the suffering Savior. Lent now has come to an end. We find ourselves in the middle of the sacred Triduum. Three days to commemorate the Passover of the Lord. His Passover to new life. His Passover to the heavenly Father. It is Good Friday.

On this day, the Church draws us into the mystery that occupies the center of the Christian religion. She points us toward the Cross of Christ: our mind and heart, body and soul — our whole beings. She places us on Calvary, "the place called the Skull" (Lk 23: 33). What do we behold? The Son of God nailed to the wood of a cross. This is no ordinary execution. The sacrifice of God's Son on the altar of the Cross enacts the first complete and perfect expression of godly worship. No wonder the French poet Charles Péguy cries out, "When one considers, O my God, when one considers, that this happened only once." "Quand on pense, mon Dieu, quand on pense que cela n'est arrivé qu'une fois…"[1] Never before anything like this. Never again will things continue exactly the same. Today we behold something altogether new. As the Church's liturgy reminds us, the sacramental life of the Church came into existence when blood and water gushed forth from the pierced side of Christ.[2] Water for Baptism, blood for the Eucharist. Since that moment, the perfect worship of God requires identification with Christ, the one Mediator. Since that moment, we are encouraged to draw water joyfully from the pierced side of our Savior. Since that moment, this Friday has always been known as a "good" Friday. God's Friday.

Because of the love and obedience that Christ demonstrated on it, the Church venerates the Cross of Christ as the sacred instrument of our salvation. She has been doing this publicly since Christians first gained freedom from repressive, persecuting governments. Throughout the world, the Church invites her faithful to show visible and explicit reverence for the wood of the Cross. During the afternoon liturgy that will follow this spiritual exercise, all present will move forward to kiss the Cross of Christ held by the bishop and his assistants. The same procession moves forward in Los Angeles, in Houston, and in Chicago. The same adoration occurs in Milan, in London, and in Paris. The same kissing of the Cross takes place in Manila, Tokyo, and Seoul. The same ritual happens in every situation where Christians are free to venerate the Cross of their Savior — in Nairobi, in Lagos, and Capetown, in Buenos Aires, and Rio de Janeiro, and Lima. On whatever continent, in whatever place, Christians continue an ancient liturgical tradition. It dates at least from the fourth century, when pilgrims to Jerusalem first enacted this Good Friday adoration. Indeed, Christians on this day have always come forward to embrace the instrument of their salvation. What else is there to do on Good Friday? After all, O my God, "this happened only once…"

Why should the Church encourage special reverence to an inert instrument of capital punishment? What is so special about pieces of crossed wood that, as it happened, were used to execute prisoners in first-century Palestine? After all, is it not a matter of "mere historical circumstance" that Jesus died on a cross? Could not Christ have been put to death by the sword? By club? By rope? Why did God surrender his Son to an agonizing and slow death instead of granting him a relatively painless and quick one? One thing is for sure: nothing escapes God's providence — not so much as a single detail of anyone's life. Surely not the life — or the death — of his only Son. Christ was crucified. That meant three hours of agony. Crucifixions work that way. They take time. Why three hours? Why crucifixion? When it comes to inquiring into God's choices, no direct answer is available to us. We do know one thing, however. The actual manner of Christ's death instructs us about divine truth. For a rule of divine pedagogy stipulates that everything Christ did or said or suffered is ordered to our instruction unto salvation. These three hours of prayer and song today invite us to undergo a divine, saving instruction, one that will draw us deeply into the mysteries of Catholic life.

Why did it suit God's saving purpose that Christ should die on a cross? When searching for an answer, we should not overlook the obvious. Death by crucifixion takes time. Why three hours of suffering? Today's devotions prompt one reply: Death by crucifixion allowed Jesus sufficient time to reflect, and

to speak. The time spent on the Cross gave Christ the chance to utter words, words of a dying man, words of God. Seven words. Seven words recorded in the canonical, that is, the authentic, Gospels. During these three hours of prayerful meditation, each of us should bear in mind an important question: What was Jesus thinking about as he hung upon the Cross? The Gospels supply the seven words, seven clues to help us discover the mind of Christ (see Phil 2: 5). And today, the Church gives us three hours to compose our answer to the question: What was Jesus thinking on the Cross? No wonder Christians always have set these three hours apart for reflection, for prayer, for sorrowing.[3] After all, we are commanded to keep among ourselves the mind which was in Christ Jesus.

First, let us consider Christ's human thoughts. The Incarnation of God in Christ means that God chooses to reveal himself through one man's human activity. This man's thoughts then were like our thoughts. It is true, of course, that Christ's thoughts were purified of all sinful distraction and disorder. Still, they were human thoughts. Thoughts like the ones that you and I turn over in our own minds: thoughts of love and caring, thoughts of sorrow, thoughts of personal relationships.

Consider a few obvious examples: Christ thought about his friends, especially those who stood by him at the Cross, just as we are wont to think about our friends. He surely thought about his mother, just as we are given to think about our mothers. He thought above all about his Father, as we should think about the heavenly Father and those who embody au-thentic paternal love. It should come as no surprise: Even on the Cross, Jesus thought thoughts that we think all the time.

There is more. Christ's human thoughts possess a dignity and power peculiar to those of a divine Person. To put it another way, although Jesus thought human thoughts, divine knowledge and love shaped these thoughts, these self-reflections, these movements of his human heart, into instruments of God's very own work. Thus, when he thought about his friends, Christ was actually thinking about each one of us — not in the abstract, but personally and by name. When he thought about his mother, Christ was really loving her as a mother for all mankind, for he knew about the world of divine love made incarnate in her womb. Finally, when he thought about his Father, Christ knew that he was obediently restoring the divine image in every man and woman. It is Christ himself who tells us this good news, when he says of us to the Father: "I have been glorified in them" (Jn 17: 10).

Jesus' love is unique. His charity as man depends directly upon his personal union with God – what theologians call the "grace of union." In a Lenten sermon that Saint Thomas Aquinas preached around 1273 in Naples, this saint whom the Church calls the Common Doctor taught that "the Lord strengthens us against temptation by the fervor of his charity, because any charity no matter how small can resist sin."[4] On the Cross, Jesus remains the divine Word of creation whose God-given charity suffices to cleanse the sins of the whole world. What was Jesus thinking about on the Cross? He was thinking that God loves us,

not because we are good, but because God himself is sheer goodness. He was thinking about our liberation from sin. He was thinking, in short, about the new creation and the divine glory that his death reveals to the world. As he tells his Father, "I glorified you on earth by accomplishing the work that you gave me to do" (Jn 17: 4). So spoke Christ on the night before he died.

Our three-hour reflection today brings together in a venerable cathedral several thousand New Yorkers and visitors from around the world—as well as many more who join us by radio. All want to discover the mind of Christ, his thoughts. So we ponder the words that Jesus speaks from the Cross. Christ's words provide mirror images of his thoughts. They are words that bring forgiveness: "Father, forgive them." They are words that announce

Christ's purpose for us: "This day you will be with me in paradise." They are words of invitation: "There is your mother." They are words that reveal sympathy with all forms of human suffering: "My God, my God, why have you forsaken me?" They are words of desire and assurance: "I thirst." They are words that announce a love that lasts for ever: "It is finished." They are words that instruct us about the most important of things in life: "Father, into your hands I commend my spirit." They are Christ's Last Words. Think! O my God! They are words spoken only once.

Notes

[1] Charles Péguy, *Le mystère de la charité de Jeanne d'Arc* (Paris, 1941), p. 49.

[2] Roman Liturgy, "Preface," Mass in Honor of the Sacred Heart of Jesus.

[3] Jesuit missionary activity in the New World apparently occasioned the start of this pious practice. The servant of God, Father Alphonsus Messia, S.J., who died in Lima on January 4, 1732, devised and practiced the devotion in Peru. The exercises began on Good Friday at midday, and continued for the three following hours. The "Three Hours" was introduced into Rome about the year 1788, and from there spread throughout the Catholic world. For further information, see *The Raccolta, or, Collection of Indulgenced Prayers & Good Works*, trans. Ambrose St. John, 10th ed. (New York: Benziger Brothers, 1924), Section, VI, no. 30.

[4] St. Thomas Aquinas, *Collationes in orationem dominicam*, quoted in *The Three Greatest Prayers: Commentaries on the Lord's Prayer, the Hail Mary, and the Apostles' Creed*, trans. Laurence Shapcote (London: Burns, Oates & Washbourne, 1937).

 FIRST WORD

When they came to the place called the Skull, they crucified him and the criminals there, one on his right, the other
on his left. Then Jesus said,

"FATHER, FORGIVE THEM, THEY KNOW NOT WHAT THEY DO."

They divided his garments by casting lots.

The people stood by and watched; the rulers, meanwhile,
sneered at him and said, "He saved others, let him save
himself if he is the chosen one, the Messiah of God."

Even the soldiers jeered at him. As they approached to offer him wine they called out, "If you are King of the Jews,
save yourself." Above him there was an inscription that
read, "This is the King of the Jews."

Lk 23: 33-38

The Betrayal and Arrest of Jesus

ather, forgive them, they know not what they do" (Lk 23: 34). The first word that Jesus speaks from his Cross is "Father." It is the same word that he spoke when he first taught the disciples to pray. "Father, hallowed be your name, your kingdom come" (Lk 11: 2). Now Christ addresses to his Father the petition of the "Our Father" that begs forgiveness. How are we to understand this first word? Theologians help unfold the mysteries of faith for our understanding. One of them already quoted, the Dominican saint and teacher Thomas Aquinas, explains Christ's plea for forgiveness as a manifestation of his love: "To show the abundance of the love which led him to suffer," Aquinas assures us, "Christ on the cross

sought pardon for his persecutors. He wished to suffer at the hands of both Jews and gentiles so that the fruit of his petition might reach them both."[1] We are left with one conclusion. When Christ asks forgiveness for those who are crucifying him, he pleads for us. Not for some of us, but for all of us. Everybody.

Thomas Aquinas got it right. His interpretation finds authoritative confirmation in the documents of the Second Vatican Council. "Christ, as the Church has always maintained and maintains, went willingly and with immense love to his Passion and death because of the sins of all men so that all may obtain salvation."[2] The Swiss theologian and cardinal Charles Journet expresses poignantly the response that Christ's plea for forgiveness should inspire in the hearts of all for whom he made it: "O Jesus, my God, make me realize from now on that it is I who made you bleed."[3]

It is impossible for us to penetrate the pathos embodied in the first word, the plea that God forgive sinners, without at the same time pondering the reversal of the divine order that human sin introduces into the world. If sin matters not a whit to us, then neither will pardon for sin. Those who do not recognize the life-order that sin destroys do not await the rectification of their transgressions. Those for whom the good means nothing do not rejoice when the good is restored. Those impervious to sin remain impervious also to forgiveness.

To enter into the mysteries of sin and forgiveness, we may recall the account of creation recorded in the Book of Genesis. There we discover that the creation of all things visible and invisible entails an ordering or design. "God looked at

everything he had made, and he found it very good" (Gn 1:31). Goodness flows from integrity. Integrity requires that everything exist in its proper relation to the Creator. Catholic faith proceeds upon the conviction (one held, moreover, through both faith and reason) that there exists an ordering between God and intelligent creatures—angels and men—and between them and everything else that exists in the material universe. The latter ordering achieves its iconic representation when God presents to Adam the animals he has created so that the "man" can name them.

"The man gave names to all the cattle, all the birds of the air, and all the wild animals" (Gn 2: 20). The prior ordering, that between God and man, is displayed in the command that God gives to our first parents not to eat of the tree of good and evil. "The Lord God gave man this order: 'You are free to eat from any of the trees of the garden except of the tree of knowledge of good and bad'" (Gn 2: 16). With this command, the human creature discovers the original divine order of things. It is an order that requires obedience. The angels also received a command. Some obeyed, whereas others rebelled.[4]

To recognize an ordered plan of creation does not require that one take sides in the evolution or intelligent design debate (although truly it is difficult not to recognize the imprint of intelligent design in the whole of creation, even if the divine intelligence includes provision for random or chance developments). Perhaps nowhere does this intelligent design, this divine plan, become more apparent than in the complex physical, psychological, and social reality that is human marriage. The Catholic view is well known: Christ's saving work is manifest in the lives of two members of Christ, at the very sources of human life, where love and abiding fidelity represent one of the most striking instances of a sacrament of the blessed Trinity precisely because marriage, like death, is an unavoidable circumstance for the human race.[5] Sadly, the contemporary and arrogant disparagement of marriage also reveals that human freedom can thwart the divine order inherent in the nature of things. Well did Blaise Pascal observe: "The elect will be ignorant of their virtues, and the reprobate of the greatness of their sins…"[6]

The simplest definition for sin comes from the pen of Thomas Aquinas. A sinful action is one deprived of its true order. The saint refers to the order of creation, the order of being, the order that derives from the Maker of heaven and earth. This divine order also embodies an order of love. Sin implies an action headed in the wrong direction. What wrong direction? The answer is simple: away from God, away from others, away from the good things that perfect us as creatures of the living God.[7]

Saint Augustine, the early-fifth-century Church Father who enormously influenced how the Church expresses her faith, referred to the divine order that inheres in everything as the eternal law: "eternal" to indicate that the order comes from God, "law" to make it clear that the universe and all who dwell within it—angels and men—remain subject to his plan, his design, his order.

It is difficult for our contemporaries to imagine that there exists a law which is not the result of agreement reached among peoples. In other words, many resent a law they did not have a hand in establishing. This difficulty opens up a trap for many of our period. They consider themselves not bound by eternal laws they did not create. Not bound, and exculpated. The fact that our contemporaries easily dismiss eternal law does not mean that God allows their dismissal. That many people ignore the Creator does not mean that the Creator rescinds his plan or design. That some people place themselves outside the order of divine wisdom does not mean that God abandons the order that governs all that exists.

Again, the most apparent instance of the divine order that God has placed in the world is marriage itself. Without marriage, the order of future generations, those who will come after us, is imperiled. Marriage, like death, remains an unavoidable circumstance of human life.

The truth that marriage is essential becomes clear when we reflect that no technological substitute exists for the procreation and rearing of children. The intelligent passage from one human generation to another reflects the primordial order that exists between the Creator and the creatures that he created. "Be fertile and multiply" (Gn 1: 28). Human beings are special. They alone can freely participate in the plan, the design, the order that is God's very own. This divine plan exceeds our wildest imagination. The Second Vatican Council sketches the Big Picture: "Indeed, the Lord Jesus, when he prayed to the Father, 'that all may be one... as we are one' (Jn 17: 21-22) opened up vistas closed to human reason, for he implied a certain likeness between the union of the divine Persons and the unity of God's sons in truth and charity. This likeness reveals that man, who is the only creature on earth which God willed for itself, cannot fully find himself except through a sincere gift of himself (cf. Lk 17: 33)."[8] Sincere gift of oneself. Marriage offers one example of how human beings can achieve this sincere gift of self.[9] There are other life vocations that equally realize the sincere gift of oneself. Whatever legitimate form it takes, the sincere gift of self remains incumbent on all people. And because we often fail in this self-giving, we all stand in need of forgiveness. Christ knew this, and so he prayed, "Father, forgive them."

Forgiveness restores divine order. There is, moreover, no secular counterpart to forgiveness born out of divine love: forbearance perhaps, even remission of debts, but not forgiveness born of love. Only Christ introduces into the world this supreme gift, at once human and divine. When Jesus begs forgiveness for his persecutors, a new order is announced. This order had been already enacted the night before he died when he took bread, said the blessing, and gave it to his disciples, saying, "This is my body, which will be given for you; do this in memory of me" (Lk

22: 19). This order had been illustrated when at the same supper, Christ washed the feet of his disciples, saying, "As I have done for you, you should also do" (Jn 13: 15). Now on Calvary, the full sacrificial character of the Eucharistic action appears. Christ dies on the Cross so that we might obtain the forgiveness of our sins.

Man needs forgiveness. There is no alternative to abiding in the order of love that God has established for the well-being of the world. God has made man a little less than the angels (see Ps 8: 6). Because our minds move slowly, we can live out a lifetime of repentance and fresh starts, of returning again and again for forgiveness. "To say that, once a person has sinned," warns Saint Thomas, "he cannot receive the gift of grace, is derogatory of divine power."[10] The first word from the Cross establishes an order within the Church of Christ that exists in no other institution, no other forum, no place else. The Church identifies her ability to forgive sins in God's name as the Power of the Keys: "And so I say to you, you are Peter, and upon this rock I will build my church, and the gates of the netherworld shall not prevail against it. I will give you the keys to the kingdom of heaven. Whatever you bind on earth shall be bound in heaven; and whatever you loose on earth shall be loosed in heaven" (Mt 16: 18-19). The reason is simple: Only God can forgive sins.

We hear the primordial prayer of Christian forgiveness from the lips of the crucified Savior of the world. This word creates an expectation. Now, every human being is called to fulfill the command of Jesus: "But to you who hear I say, love your enemies, do good to those who hate you…" (Lk 6: 27). The only alternative to forgiveness is destruction: the end of oneself and of the unforgiven other. Everyday occurrences throughout the world bear startling testimony to what happens when brother remains set unforgivingly against brother. To forgive every offense characterizes the saint. We grow in sanctity by loving the heavenly Father, who makes his sun rise on the bad and the good, and who causes rain to fall on the just and the unjust. In the Christian family, children begin to learn about authentic forgiveness from parents who love each other. This formation is imperative. For each new generation must come to discover the form of love that Christ alone introduces into the world when he cries out, "Father, forgive them."

Notes

[1] St. Thomas Aquinas, *Summa theologiae* III, q. 47, art. 4, ad 1 (Blackfriars edition, 1965, trans. Richard T. R. Murphy, O.P.).

[2] Second Vatican Council, Declaration on the Church's Relation to Non-Christian Religions, *Nostra aetate* 4, in *Decrees of the Ecumenical Councils*, vol. 2, *Trent to Vatican II*, ed. Norman P. Tanner (Washington, D.C.: Sheed & Ward/Georgetown University Press, 1990), p. *971.

[3] Charles Journet, *Les sept paroles du Christ en croix* (Paris: Editions du Seuil, 1952), p. 52; translation is mine.

[4] Those angels who sinned learned the hard lesson in a moment of disobedient choice. Because of their unique intelligence and gifts of nature, the angels are confirmed as sinners or saints by one act of the will: for the bad angels, rebellion; for the good ones, obedience.

[5] For further discussion, see Colman E. O'Neill, O.P., *Sacramental Realism* (Chicago: MidWest Theological Forum, 1998), pp. 187–92.

[6] Blaise Pascal, *Pensées*, trans. W. F. Trotter (New York: E. P. Dutton & Co., 1958), no. 514 (ed. Brunschvicg, no. 515).

[7] The Old Testament presents a compelling image of an action deprived of its due order. The prophet Hosea is asked to take for himself an adulteress to demonstrate Israel's infidelity toward God: "Even as the Lord loves the people of Israel, though they turn to other gods and are fond of raisin cakes" (Hos 3: 1). Adultery occurs when a spouse moves away from the embrace of the one who by mutual consent has become the irreplaceable other. Fidelity is not a moral value added on to marriage. Marital fidelity is built into the very nature of what makes marriage to be marriage: "the partnership of the whole of life" (see *Codex Iuris Canonici*, canon 1055 §1). When the intimate acts proper to spouses take place outside of the fidelity promised at marriage, these acts lack their due ordering. When this happens, we find a paradigmatic instance of sin. So God compares unfaithful and apostate Israel to an adulteress, and he even sends a special prophet to enact the lesson dramatically. Raisin cakes were considered aphrodisiacal, and were associated with fertility rites and goddess worship. Wayward Israel had become fond of them.

[8] Second Vatican Council, Pastoral Constitution on the Church in the Modern World, *Gaudium et spes*, no. 24.

[9] Pope John Paul II comments on what the gift of self in marriage entails: "Conjugal love involves a totality, in which all the elements of the person enter—appeal of the body and instinct, power of feeling and affectivity, aspiration of the spirit and of will. It aims at a deeply personal unity, the unity that, beyond union in one flesh, leads to forming one heart and soul; it demands indissolubility and faithfulness in definitive mutual giving; and is open to fertility." The text comes from an address that the Holy Father gave to the delegates of the Centre de Liaison des Équipes de Recherche on November 3, 1979, and it is repeated in *Familiaris consortio* 13.

[10] St. Thomas Aquinas, *Compendium theologiae*, trans. Cyril Vollert, S.J. (St. Louis: B. Herder Book Company, 1947), pp. 154, 155.

$\mathcal{S}$ECOND WORD

Now one of the criminals hanging there reviled Jesus, saying, "Are you not the Messiah? Save yourself and us."

The other, however, rebuking him, said in reply, "Have you no fear of God, for you are subject to the same condemnation? And indeed, we have been condemned justly, for the sentence we received corresponds to our crimes, but this man has done nothing criminal."

Then he said, "Jesus, remember me when you come into your kingdom."

He replied to him,

"AMEN, I SAY TO YOU, TODAY YOU WILL BE WITH ME IN PARADISE."

Lk 23: 39-43

The Descent into Hell

men, I say to you, today you will be with me in Paradise" (Lk 23: 43). Paradise. The word originally means royal park or enclosure.[1] From the Cross, Christ promises entrance into paradise to a man whom we have come to know as the Good Thief. Christ responds to the man's plaintive cry: "Jesus, remember me when you come into your kingdom" (Lk 23: 42). So much have Christians throughout the ages loved this anonymous malefactor that the tradition has given him a name, Dismas. The man whom Jesus addresses thwarted the divine plan for human life. The seventh commandment, "You shall not steal" (Ex 20: 15), expresses the design or order that Dismas flouted or ignored.

Instead of earning his livelihood by honest labor, he had given himself over to a life of brigandry. Most people recognize the common — the natural — sense embedded in the seventh commandment. Who among us would create a society where nothing forbids that another take by stealth or force what one needs to live? The brigands of the ancient world posed an enormous threat to civilized life. They formed parallel communities, often retreating to inaccessible mountainous regions; from there they preyed on decent folk. This disordered pattern of brigandry still exists today in places. In any case, to one of these scoundrels, these brigands, Christ turns and speaks a word of beatification: "Today you will be with me in Paradise."

Yes! Great mystery of divine providence. The Good Thief discovers a way to beatitude. He is made happy. There is no explanation given for the sudden reversal of eternal fortune that befalls Dismas. Why him, and not the other man? We do not know. No one knows. "For who can say by what strange way / Christ brings his will to light…"[2] All that we know is that Christ heard the reproach Dismas spoke to the other thief: "Have you no fear of God, for you are subject to the same condemnation? And indeed, we have been condemned justly, for the sentence we received corresponds to our crimes" (Lk 23: 40-41). Still, we are left with the question: What moved Dismas to accept capital punishment as a just recompense for his sins? Did

he recognize that his thievery destroyed the right ordering that human society requires to survive peacefully? Maybe. What is more important, who informed the Good Thief that there exists a place — "your kingdom" — where no disorder exists? And why, moreover, would Dismas have wanted to go there? In short, the question remains, what made the Good Thief good? It is not easy to know. And the Church supplies no authoritative statement. "For who can say by what strange way / Christ brings his will to light…?" At the same time, the instinct of faith compels us to acknowledge that behind the scenes, as it were, God was all the time acting in some "strange way."

What explains Dismas's conversion? What emboldened him?

Today you will be with me in Paradise.

What made him look upon Christ as a friend? Again, we possess no revealed explanation. But the Christian imagination strains to supply one. It seeks to answer the question, "What disposed this thief to turn to Christ and to ask for his forgiveness?" The question presents itself because we cannot escape the burden of freedom. Salvation is freely given. It also is freely received. God does not treat us like automatons. Only one of those crucified with Jesus receives the promise. So Dismas had to have been moved to seek the gift of forgiveness, and he had to have been moved to receive it. What moved him? Surely there is no reason to suppose it was his virtuous life… How then did Dismas merit his first and final grace?

Though they do not come to us wearing the authoritative mantle of Scripture, apocryphal stories—stories whose origin is hidden or uncertain—sometimes contain a kernel of truth. There is an apocryphal explanation for Dismas's last-minute beatification. It begins with the assumption that Calvary was not the first time or place that Dismas encountered Christ. It is said that a young Dismas first met the Holy Family in other circumstances, perhaps during the flight into Egypt. Dismas appears in these accounts as a young boy already attached to a band of brigands. The young Dismas, it is said, became moved by the beauty, gentleness, and love that radiated from the Mother and her Child. Saints have even gone on to hypothesize that the Blessed Mother on Calvary recognized Dismas. She remembered the lad who had once upon a time shown her gentle consideration. Is it far-fetched to think that the young Dismas had glimpsed just for a minute the primordial bond of love between mother and child, an order and bond that he may not have experienced for himself? The saints further suppose that Mary at the foot of the Cross asked Christ—on the spot—for Dismas's conversion. Ah! There is a cause of meriting.[3] There is an answer to our question. Then we return to the authentic Gospel account. "This day... Paradise." The apocryphal explanation for Dismas's conversion is less important than the message that it aims to communicate. This message is clear. In every good thing that happens in our lives, God acts first.

We learn from the Good Thief about the way that God makes his desire to save all men work efficaciously in the world. We are never alone. Someone always is praying for us. Others merit for us. That's how it works in the Church. God works through an ordering, an ordering of

holy persons to save us. At the head of this ordering stands Christ. The pattern is called mediation. Seeing this divine mediation manifested in the Good Thief should console us. At the same time, the predestination of Dismas should not distract us from the horror of Calvary.

Crucifixion represents cruel and unusual punishment. The earliest Christians declined to represent Christ on the Cross. They had witnessed the devastating spectacle of crucifixion, and were unwilling to display the Savior of the world suffering a punishment that so degrades human dignity.[4] There were three men crucified, says Saint Augustine: one who is Savior, another who is to be saved, and a third who is to be damned. Each is equal in punishment received but unequal in the cause for receiving the punishment.[5] Christ is the one crucified without cause, the innocent lamb. No wonder the Christian imagination sought to explain historically the origins of the good fortune that befell Dismas to explain his mediation.

When Dismas asks to come into Christ's kingdom, he seeks not a place but a relationship. The kingdom of God is a place where love reigns. Not any  kind of love. Love in the truth. For this teaching, we enjoy the authority of the Apostle to the Gentiles, Saint Paul. He reminds the Galatians that what matters for our eternal happiness, our beatitude, our entrance into the kingdom of God, is faith — that is, God's truth — "working through love" (Gal 5: 6). In Christian usage, paradise means the enclosed garden of the eternal King. What is enclosed? Not space, but an order: the order of love without blemish of the least disorder. What explains the fact that an anonymous criminal executed in first-century Palestine for crimes that were commonplace at the time attains a place in the Gospel account of salvation? The answer is clear: God wants us to recognize ourselves in the Good Thief. He wants us to know that whatever our departure from his saving plan, our thwarting of his wise design, our rejection of his loving order may take or have taken in our lives, we can still cry out, "Jesus, remember me when you come into your kingdom" (Lk 23: 42).

The Jesuit poet Gerard Manley Hopkins translated a hymn that has formed part of Christian worship for centuries, the *Adoro Te Devote* "Godhead here in hiding, whom I do adore." The hymn celebrates the Eucharist. Saint Thomas Aquinas composed the Latin text for Corpus Christi, the festival in early summer that we call the Solemnity of the Body and Blood of Christ. One strophe mentions Dismas. Aquinas places us at once on Calvary and before the Eucharist. "On the cross Thy godhead made no sign to men, / Here Thy very manhood steals from human ken: / Both are my confession, both are my belief, / And I pray the prayer of the dying thief." Remember me…

Only Christ can ensure entrance into the enclosed garden of the King. Only God can promise man paradise. Only God creates paradise. For "God is love, and whoever remains in love remains in God and God in him" (1 Jn 4: 16). No wonder that Pope Benedict XVI in his first encyclical introduces his theme, *Deus caritas est*, "God is Love," by citing these words from the First Letter of John: They "express," the Pope tells us, "with remarkable clarity the heart of the Christian faith: the Christian image of God and the resulting image of mankind and its destiny."[6] Dismas the executed thief. Dismas the repentant thief. Dismas the Good Thief. He represents each of us. We are made in the image of God. We must love. Our destiny is to love. Happy lives are constructed by loving truthfully. Faith working through love leads to paradise. The vision becomes glorious. But there is more. When our loving fails, we are not left without recourse. We can turn and cry out wholeheartedly, "Jesus, remember me when you come into your kingdom." The great assurance that Good Friday brings to the Christian world is that Jesus always turns back to us and says, "Today you will be with me in Paradise."

A Spanish poem from about 1625, Calderón de la Barca's *La* *devoción de la Cruz*, captures the overall grace of the Good Thief: "O holy Cross, I have always prayed spontaneously, and with so much faith, do not let me die without confession. Look! At least I am not the first sinner who, on you, O holy Cross, has confided myself to God."[7]

Notes

[1] The use here of the word "paradise," from the Greek word παράδεισος, meaning a king's royal park or enclosure, calls to mind the garden of Eden in Genesis 2 and 3.

[2] Oscar Wilde, "The Ballad of Reading Gaol," IV, in *The Ballad of Reading Gaol* (London: Leonard Smithers, 1898), p. 23.

[3] See St. Thomas Aquinas, *Summa theologiae* I-II, q. 114, art. 6: "No one can merit the first grace for someone else by the merit of strict equivalence (condign) but Christ alone."

[4] See M. J. Lagrange, O.P., *L'Evangile de Jésus-Christ* (Paris, 1928), p. 565.

[5] St. Augustine, *Enarrationes in Psalmos* XXXIV, sermon 2, no. 1.

[6] Encyclical Letter of Pope Benedict XVI, *Deus caritas est*, no. 1.

[7] Pedro Calderón de la Barca, Comedias, *La devoción de la Cruz*, Third Day, scene XI: "Mi natural devoción / Siempre os pidió con fe tanta, / No permitieseis, Cruz santa, / Muriese sin confession. / No serè el primer ladron / Que en vos se confiese à Dios" in *Devotion to the Cross in Six Plays*, trans. E. Honig (New York: Fordham University Press, 1996).

$\mathcal{T}$HIRD WORD

Standing by the cross of Jesus were his mother and his mother's sister, Mary the wife of Clopas, and Mary of Magdala.

When Jesus saw his mother and the disciple there whom he loved, he said to his mother,

"WOMAN, BEHOLD, YOUR SON."

Then he said to the disciple,

"BEHOLD, YOUR MOTHER."

And from that hour the disciple took her into his home.

Jn 19: 25-27

Mary and John at the Cross of Jesus

"Woman, behold, your son." "Behold, your mother." From the Cross, the dying Christ provides for an order that is as intimate as it is personal: the relationship between a mother and her child. The Gospel of John captures the setting for this exchange between Christ and his mother and between Christ and John,

the Beloved Disciple. "When Jesus saw his mother and the disciple there whom he loved, he said to his mother, 'Woman, behold, your son'" (Jn 19: 26). The Passion according to John is read on Good Fridays throughout the Catholic world. Christ's third word is meant to create in us an expectation of belonging. When he provides for his mother, the Savior also provides for us. So the Catholic world attaches to this day an adjective that captures the sentiment of the graces that we receive. Language groups variously describe the Friday on which Christ died. The Germans call today "Dear Friday"; the French, Italian, and Spanish, "Holy Friday"; the English-speaking world, "Good Friday."

What makes this Friday so dear, so holy, so good? We can turn to the Gospel of John, the fourth Gospel, to provide an answer. For only there do we find Christ's word to the disciple whom he loved: "Behold, your mother." For the Christian believer, this remark brings a special consolation. One of Christ's own disciples—his friend—becomes the first person to discover existentially what makes Good Friday good. John the Evangelist receives the Blessed Virgin Mary.

"From that hour the disciple took her into his home" (Jn 19: 27). She is no ordinary woman, but the woman in whom everything that the Church will become already flourishes. It is Mary who first em-  bodies the dearness, the holiness, the goodness of the redemption accomplished by her Son on Good Friday.

No wonder the Church so much esteems the Gospel according to John: "The Gospels," wrote Origen, a Church Father with a strong Catholic imagination, "are the first fruit of all Scripture and the Gospel of John is the first of all Gospels: No one can grasp its meaning without having leaned his head on Jesus' breast and having received from Jesus, Mary as his mother."[1] Origen expresses a truth that will be repeated throughout the Christian centuries: Only Mary introduces us into the mystery of divine love that Jesus creates on the Cross. Observe, for instance, that in churches, her image and altar ordinarily occupy a place close to where Christ's sacrifice is daily offered. Such is the case here at Saint Patrick's Cathedral, where the Mary chapel stands directly behind the main sanctuary.

The liturgy from an ancient Church of the East helps us to enter into Our Lady's experience of the drama of Calvary. In a hymn (that once may have formed part of a liturgical drama, that is to say, a much earlier version of today's service), we hear words spoken by Mary at the very moment when she encounters Jesus on his way to Jerusalem: "Wither goest thou, my Son? Wherefore this hurried step? Is it to a second marriage feast at Cana that thou thus hastenest, there to turn water into wine? Must I come with thee my Son?"[2] Christ's answer to this question is delivered from the Cross. It is his third word: "Woman, there is your son." Mary indeed must accompany Christ to the place where the wine of the Last Supper achieves its once and for all saving efficaciousness. And there she discovers the full dimension of her being, of her mission as Mother of the Redeemer. Mary's new motherhood derives from the new love which achieved definitive maturity at the foot of the Cross. There she shares deeply in the redemptive love and sufferings of her Son. No wonder the Church proclaims Mary, Mother of Christ and mother of mankind.[3]

"Woman, there is your son." When Christ speaks this word, he is thinking about the people of the world. No one is excluded from Christ's salvific purpose. So also, no one is excluded from becoming a son or daughter of Mary. From the moment that Mary is confided to the care of the disciple Jesus loved, each Christian man and woman becomes definitively a child of Mary. The Fathers of the Church, with their flare for seeing the complete picture of Catholic doctrine, loved to contrast the Blessed Virgin Mary with the first woman, Eve, "the mother of all the living" (Gn 3: 20). Mary is called the New Eve. Whereas Eve contributed to the death of the human race, Mary participates in the restoration of the order of life. Eve participates in the first sin, the original sin, the sin that introduced disorder into the world. We call it the sin of nature. Why? Because unlike personal sin, which belongs to the one who commits it, original sin affects all who share the same human nature as Adam and Eve.

Sometimes people wonder why the whole race should suffer for the sin of the first parents. The question loses some of its urgency when Christ addresses John, and says, "Behold, your mother." Had we been left with the life that Eve transmitted, our lives would have been much different than they are. Perhaps there would have been reason for complaint. Mary eliminates all cause for complaint. "The knot of Eve's disobedience was untied through the obedience of Mary; what the virgin Eve had bound through her lack of faith, the virgin Mary untied by her faith."[4] So Mary becomes the true mother of the living. As Saint Paul assures us, "whoever is in Christ is a new creation: the old things have passed away; behold, new things have come" (2 Cor 5: 17). Mary ranks first among the new things that have come into existence because of Christ's death. So she is able to beget others in this new life. Mary is "clearly mother of the members [of Christ] . . . for she has cooperated with love in the birth of the faithful in the Church, who are members of its Head."[5]

Now at the hour of the Cross, Christ fulfills the work that the Father gave him to accomplish. The tenderness with which Mary cared for the child Jesus becomes compassion for those who are the fruit of his saving work. Mary loves all those whom Jesus saves by his death on the Cross. She "is perfectly united with Christ in his self-emptying." [6] And like a good mother, Mary sustains our obedience of faith. Saint Thomas Aquinas also takes up the patristic theme of Eve and Mary. "Eve," he writes, "sought the fruit, but did not find there what she wished for. In her fruit the blessed Virgin found all that Eve had wanted."[7] We know who is the fruit of Mary's womb: Jesus. Eve met disappointment. Instead of blessedness came shame, confusion, and the progressive destruction of the order that God established for the well-being of his creatures. This disorder first appears blatantly when Cain slays Abel. Abel the Just. He is a figure of Christ, who from the Cross announces Mary's special role in the Church. We call it the grace of her "maternal mediation."[8] "She is a mother to us in the order of grace."[9] Mary's maternal mediation embraces the Church. No grace reaches any person on earth apart from Mary's personal love for the brothers and sisters of her only Son. This is why the saints strongly encourage us always to approach Jesus through Mary.

There are many reasons why the Christian people turn to Mary as they would turn to a mother. This filial instinct occurs spontaneously. Think of the way that a nursing child falls to its mother's breast. The movement flows instinctually from within the infant in such a way that the order of mother to child remains unmistakable. What do we behold? Tenderness. Compassion. Sustenance. These are some of the human values that maternal love embodies. Each represents a spiritual gift that the Blessed Virgin Mary communicates to her spiritual children. It is almost impossible to count the various representations of the Madonna and Child. There is the Virgin of Tenderness. There is Our Lady of Compassion. There is Mary, Mother of the Eucharist. The supreme sustenance. The variety of the portrayals displays the ways that Mary mediates the grace of Christ. There is the Christmas Madonna. She recalls the promise made by the angel to Saint Joseph: "She will bear a son and you are to name him Jesus, because he will save his people from their sins" (Mt 1: 21). There is also the Pietá. There Mary encourages us to embrace the price of our redemption from sin.

Consider Christ's first three words from the Cross. Pardon. Beatification. And now provision. Three words spoken, and Christ has yet to refer to his own sufferings. Instead, he takes care to forgive, to welcome, and to provide us with his mother. O

Blessed Virgin Mary, "Most blessed are you among women, and blessed is the fruit of your womb" (Lk 1: 42). Jesus! Blessed is your Son who brings us true happiness.

Notes

[1] Origen, *Commentary on John (In Joan.)* I, 6 (Patrologia Graeca 14:31); as quoted by Pope John Paul II in his Encyclical Letter *Mother of the Redeemer (Redemptoris Mater)*, no. 23, Vatican translation, Daughters of St. Paul edition.

[2] From an ancient Greek hymn for the Parasceve. See http://www.intermirifica.org/lent/gfhymn.htm

[3] See *Redemptoris Mater*, no. 23.

[4] See this text from St. Irenaeus, *Adversus haereses* III, 22, 4, as cited in the Dogmatic Constitution on the Church *Lumen gentium*, no. 56, note 6 (Tanner edition, p. *893).

[5] St. Augustine, *De sancta virginitate* 6 (Patrologia Latina 40, 309), as cited in *Lumen gentium*, no. 54 (Tanner edition, p. *892).

[6] *Redemptoris Mater*, no. 18.

[7] St. Thomas Aquinas, *Exposition on the Hail Mary*, in *The Three Greatest Prayers: Commentaries on the Lord's Prayer, the Hail Mary, and the Apostles' Creed*, trans. Laurence Shapcote (London: Burns, Oates & Washbourne, 1937).

[8] See *Redemptoris Mater*, nos. 38, 39.

[9] *Redemptoris Mater*, no. 38, citing *Lumen gentium*, no. 61.

FOURTH WORD

From noon onward, darkness came over the whole land until three in the afternoon.

And about three o'clock Jesus cried out in a loud voice, *"Eli, Eli, lema sabachthani?"* which means,

"MY GOD, MY GOD, WHY HAVE YOU FORSAKEN ME?"

Some of the bystanders who heard it said, "This one is calling for Elijah." Immediately one of them ran to get a sponge; he soaked it in wine, and putting it on a reed, gave it to him to drink. But the rest said, "Wait, let us see if Elijah comes to save him."

Mt 27: 45-49

Mary Receives the Body of Jesus

"y God, my God, why have you forsaken me?" (Mt 27: 46 and Mk 15: 34). The Gospels of Matthew and Mark both show us Jesus crying out to his Father these words from Psalm 22. Intense sufferings accompany Jesus' acceptance of the will of his heavenly Father. "My Father, if it is not possible that this cup pass without my drinking it, your will be done!" (Mt 26: 42). Christ's moral sufferings include the human cry of abandonment that crystallizes the acceptance of his death as redemptive. It is important for us to understand the nature of this suffering. The cry of abandonment from the Cross expresses a human sentiment that Jesus felt but not a reasoned conviction that he held. Saint Catherine of Siena, Doctor of

the Church, provides our authority. Heavenly beatitude and earthly sorrow, she assures us, can coexist in the same person.[1] Why then does Jesus vocalize his sorrow? He wants us to believe beyond all doubt that, whatever dark sentiments may envelop our hearts and minds, nothing can "separate us from the love of God" (Rom 8: 39).

Today the altars of the world stand bare. In place of the Eucharistic action, the Church will center her liturgy around Scripture readings, especially the Passion narrative, solemn petitions, and the veneration of the Cross. The reception of Holy Communion concludes the Good Friday liturgical service for which these Three Hours provide a suitable preparation. Still, today there is no Mass. No Eucharistic action. No sacrifice. We face something of an apparent paradox. The Church today commemorates the "once and for all" sacrifice of the New Law, Christ's sacrifice on the Cross, his atoning death. At the same time, the Church refrains from celebrating the true, sacramental re-enactment of her atonement. The bishop, instead of taking bread and wine, today holds up the Cross. Christian history supports the practice. As early as the third century, the astute Christian theologian Tertullian explained: "It is not fitting that we should celebrate a feast on the day on which the bridegroom is taken from us." Yet today remains that day the world still calls dear, holy, good. Kar Freitag. Vendredi saint. Good Friday.

In a celebrated woodcut,

Albrecht Dürer (1471-1528) captures an essential moment of the three hours that Jesus hung on the Cross. The artist pictures Mary Magdalene prostrate at the foot of the Cross. She is kissing the feet of Jesus. But the sixteenth-century engraver portrays the face of Christ so as to prompt the question, "Who is kissing whom?"

If we consider another ancient liturgical text, this one from the fourth century, we are led to conclude that, clearly, Christ kisses the Magdalene. An ancient Good Friday text instructs believers to cry out: "O beloved Spouse of souls, kiss us at this hour from thy Cross, for the Cross is the trophy of thy victory."[2] The trophy of Christ's victory! Wherein the victory? The answer is found in Christ's human will.

Christ's obedient love at once reveals his submission to the Father and restores to the human race the divine friendship lost through Adam's sin. This is the unique and sacred moment when the victorious Christ creates in the world a new order of fruitful love. Again we face a seeming paradox. This new order created out of the blood and the water and the cry of abandonment the Church regards as superior to whatever order would have been lived out by a sinless Adam. So the Church sings, "What good would life have been to us, had Christ not come as our Redeemer."[3] It is better for us to be restored than not to have needed restoration. Only the Catholic faith makes bold to proclaim this realistic truth and consoling mystery.

This restoration reaches everywhere. Wherever Christians adore the Cross, there the restoration happens. In diocesan presbyterates, Christ from the Cross sustains the life and ministry of his bishops and priests; in religious communities and other institutes of consecrated life, Christ from the Cross sustains the contemplation and sacrifice that should characterize their daily routines; in Christian families, Christ from the Cross sustains the *consortium totius vitae*, "the partnership of the whole of life" that distinguishes the chaste love of husband and wife.[4] To those who embrace faithfully his Cross, Christ restores divine friendship. How does the Savior accomplish this restoration? In a word, he kisses us. Christ kisses us with the power of his divinity. "O Almighty God, our Jesus," continues the fourth-century liturgical text, "kiss us, we beseech thee, Beloved Lord, who didst triumphantly return to the Father with whom thou wast and art, for ever one."[5]

The Church firmly believes that Christ's triumph is complete and that it signals the effective start of the new creation. The Letter to the Hebrews makes the point with great insistence: "But when Christ had offered for all time a single sacrifice for sins, he sat down at the right hand of God… For by a single offering he has perfected for all time those who are sanctified" (Heb 10: 12, 14). No human being escapes the need to enter into Christ's perfect sacrifice. At the start of the eighteenth century, Saint Louis-Marie Grignon de Montfort, a great apostle of Our Lady, urged his hearers to recognize this truth when he candidly described our personal dispositions outside the new order that Christ's sacrifice creates. "We are naturally prouder than peacocks, more groveling than toads, more vile than unclean animals, more envious than serpents, more gluttonous than hogs, more furious than tigers, lazier than tortoises, weaker than reeds, and more capricious than weathercocks. We have within ourselves nothing but nothingness and sin."[6]

Louis de Montfort harbored no illusions about sinful man. What separates him from postmodern nihilists? The saint confessed the power of Christ's victory. De Montfort believed in our restoration. He believed in the new creation. He believed in the power of Christ's kiss. The saint's striking psychological portrait of unredeemed nature is meant to console, not to depress and crush the human spirit. Whatever our personal states; whatever our conditions according to the flesh; whatever, even, our dispositions toward attaining holiness, Christ touches them. He transforms them. He makes them all new. The kiss of Christ illumines our minds so that we come to see the truth. It strengthens our wills so that we love the good. It even envelops our emotions so that, in faith, we experience the order and, yes, the tranquility of Christ's own rectitude. Thus at each Mass, the Church prays: "May we come to share in the divinity of Christ, who humbled himself to share in our humanity."[7]

Some theologians prefer to see in the cry of abandonment a change in Christ's divine status or in his prerogatives as a divine Person. The authentic Catholic tradition observes modesty. Saint Thomas Aquinas tells us that "God abandoned Christ in death inasmuch as he exposed him to the power of his persecutors. He withdrew his protection, but maintained the union."[8] God maintained the union. Saint Thomas refers to what the Church calls the hypostatic union, which means that in Christ "there is but one person, which is our Lord Jesus Christ, one of the Trinity."[9] The cry of abandonment does not affect Christ's divinity, for even his sufferings, including his mental anguish, while experienced in his human nature, are sustained by his immutable divine Person. So the ancient councils of the Church that deliberated on this question came to the conclusion that "he who was crucified in the flesh, our Lord Jesus Christ, is true God, Lord of glory, and one of the Holy Trinity."[10]

If we reflect for a moment, no other explanation of Christ's abandonment is possible. We are now devoting three hours to praying and meditating on Christ's seven last words. If the cry of abandonment signaled that Christ had suffered defeat or, what would be the equivalent, a dissolution of his divinity, why would the Church commemorate Good Friday? It would make better sense to forget this day. If Christ gave up on the Cross, there would be no reason to recall solemnly the three hours he hung upon it. Why would the Church hold up the Cross for our meditation and veneration if it became the instrument that finally persuaded Christ to renounce his divine mission? Why would anyone seek to unite themselves to the suffering Christ if the suffering Christ were at the same time the despairing Christ? Who would beseech Christ

to kiss them from the Cross, if the kiss were to come from a man who had abandoned all hope of embracing God? But we know that union with the suffering Christ symbolized by the kiss is precisely what the Church urges upon us, and especially on Dear Friday, on Holy Friday, on Good Friday. She urges us to receive, at the foot of the Cross, the "sacrament" of Good Friday. Let Jesus kiss you from the Cross. "O beloved Spouse of souls, kiss us at this hour from thy Cross."

In truth, Jesus does kiss us. From the Cross, the Innocent One, the Lamb without blemish, embraces his own suffering, mystical Body. From this embrace of love springs his cry of abandonment. The great Jesuit saint and Doctor of the Church, Robert Bellarmine, opined that Christ gave witness to his feeling of abandonment "so that all might understand the great price of our Redemption."[11] The point is well made. By his cry of abandonment, Christ is telling us something about ourselves. He is telling us how costly comes the price for our restoration.

What should we learn from the cry of abandonment? Again, the Easter liturgy provides the reply: "Father, how wonderful your care for us! / How boundless your merciful love! / To ransom a slave / you gave away your Son."[12] Ransom. Redemption.

We are bought back. What does this mean? The answer is simple. Wheresoever sin runs deep in our souls, Jesus heals it. The Passion of Christ, we are told, contains all the virtues and so it can heal every wound of sin. Arrogance and rebellion: the obedience of Christ heals us. Ambition and self-seeking: the humility of Christ heals us. Unchastity and immoderateness of all kinds: the patience of Christ heals us. All these virtues flow from the One who cries out from the Cross, "My God, my God, why have you forsaken me?"

Notes

1. St. Catherine of Siena, *Libro della divina dottrina* (Bari, 1912), chap. 78, p. 152: "Era beato e doloroso."

2. From a text used in the Gallican Rite for the Liturgy of the Hours at midday that dates from the fourth century.

3. Roman Liturgy, Easter Proclamation (*Exsultet*).

4. See *Codex Iuris Canonici*, canon 1055 §1.

5. From the same fourth-century text mentioned above.

6. St. Louis de Montfort, *True Devotion to Mary*, trans. Frederick William Faber (Rockford, IL: Tan Books and Publishers Inc., 1941), p. 49.

7. *Roman Missal*, Preparation of the altar and the gifts.

8. St. Thomas Aquinas, *Summa theologiae* III, q. 50, art. 2, ad 1.

9. Second Council of Constantinople (553), as quoted in the *Catechism of the Catholic Church* (CCC) 468.

10. Second Council of Constantinople (553), as quoted in CCC 468.

11. St. Robert Bellarmine, "De Septem Verbis Domini," *Opera Omnia* (Naples, 1862), vol. VI, p. 418.

12. Roman Liturgy, Easter Proclamation (*Exsultet*).

$\mathscr{F}$IFTH WORD

After this, aware that everything was now finished, in order that the scripture might be fulfilled, Jesus said,

"I THIRST."

There was a vessel filled with common wine. So they put a sponge soaked in wine on a sprig of hyssop and put it up to his mouth.

Jn 19: 28-29

The Appearance of the Risen Jesus on the Road to Emmaus

I thirst" (Jn 19: 28). Crucifixion, with its loss of blood, dehydrates the condemned man. He suffers physically. So Christ's fifth word is not unexpected. "I thirst." With a practical unanimity, spiritual authors of every period tell us that Christ thirsts for more than something liquid to drink. His real thirst is for souls. The suffer-  ing, parched Lord proclaims that he thirsts for the salvation of the world. Thomas Aquinas represents one of many witnesses to make the point. This thirst, says Aquinas, expresses Christ's "ardent desire for the salvation of the human race."[1] Today the Church speaks of the universal call to holiness.

Catholic faith always remains eminently personal. So when we hear Jesus cry out, "I thirst," we should think first of all about ourselves. Jesus thirsts very much for my soul. He wants me. This instinct betrays neither selfishness nor egoism. This very Catholic instinct rather reflects the order of charity. We see this ordering in the two great commandments that govern true religion: First, "You shall love the Lord, your God, with all your heart, with all your soul, and with all your mind." Then comes the command to love oneself: "You shall love your neighbor as yourself" (Mt 22: 37, 39).

Jesus thirsts for souls. Even on his Cross, the suffering Lord manifests himself as the Good Shepherd. Christ's own words give evidence of his pastoral solicitude: "I am the good shepherd. A good shepherd lays down his life for the sheep" (Jn 10: 11). What does it mean that he "lays down his life for the sheep"? It means that Christ's death brings new life, a new self, a new creation to the poor banished children of Eve. At the same time, his death introduces a new order into the world. A new sacramental order. From the pierced side of Christ flow blood and water, the source of the Church's sacramental life. Yes, Jesus thirsts. He thirsts for those who have been reborn into the new life that Baptism confers. He thirsts also for those who still await receiving the Gospel, who still wait for the sacraments of new life.

From the wood of a cross sanctified by his blood, God's own Son expresses the purpose of his becoming man. Jesus, one like us in all things but sin, thirsts for the souls of those whom he came to save. Who are they? The answer is simple: everybody. He came to save everybody, beginning with Adam. Salvation is a reciprocal exercise. Jesus wants to love us, and he also wants us to love him in return. So he thirsts. The thirst that Jesus experiences at his death endures throughout the ages. He thirsts for everybody who now lives, and for everybody who will come into the world until the end of time. Everybody. This last word of Jesus provides a first word for every Christian: "We love because he first loved us" (1 Jn 4: 19). "I thirst!" The priority of the divine initiative takes on human expression in these two words of a dying, dehydrated, and therefore thirsty man.

I thirst.

Christians, sometimes heroically, satisfy Christ's thirst. Many in the Church will marry, like the Venerable Pierre Toussaint, who lies buried in the crypt of this cathedral; others will devote themselves—like Blessed Mother Teresa of Calcutta, or New York's own Sisters of Life—to a life of consecrated witness to Christ's love and glory; and some men will make the sacrifice of family and fortune to become priests. These will become bound to Christ himself. The Church uses the impressive word "ontological" to stress the reality of the bond: these men will become other Christs. They will become shepherds of those souls for whom Jesus thirsts. Whether lay, consecrated, or ordained, all believers form one body in Christ and live in him one holiness, though in three distinctive circles of ecclesial communion. One Lord, one faith, one baptism! Baptism. This is the sacrament whose reception above all satisfies Christ's thirst. This holy and life-giving sacrament gives human creatures a share in the divine life and so makes of them friends of God. "Our fellowship," Saint John assures us, "is with the Father and with his Son, Jesus Christ" (1 Jn 1: 3). What does it mean to say that Christ thirsts for our souls? The answer is simple. He wants us to be his friends.

Is it proper to dwell on Good Friday on Christ's thirst for souls, on the Catholic vocations that satisfy this thirst, instead of dwelling on his actual suffering from thirst? Does this meditation distract us from remembering Christ's afflictions? The saints do not think so. So they encourage us to ponder devoutly the "ardent desire" that Christ's thirst represents. Christ's physical thirst also moves us to return to the question, "Why did

Christ die on a cross?" It took a long and painful time for Christ to die. He had time to become thirsty. He had time to conceive his "ardent desire." He had time to desire your soul and mine. What does the thirsting Lord desire? Christ desires that we comprehend how much he loves us, how much he wants to give us the new life of grace. This new life of grace, this new order of grace, Saint Paul recognizes simply as Christ's Body, the Church.

In 2008, the Archdiocese of New York celebrates two hundred years of Catholic life as a diocese. In order for the life of the diocese to continue, some Catholic men who are suitably disposed must make the sacrifice of celibacy in order to serve as priests. It is incumbent on those whom God calls as shepherds of souls to help slake the thirst of Jesus. They must announce the Gospel and they must baptize. They must forgive the sins of the baptized. They must celebrate the Eucharist. They must care for the dying and bury the dead. Further, they must be instruments of the sacramental economy for those persons who still do not know what it means that Christ died for them. Which man can commit himself to the wholehearted celibate work of pastoral charity without being fully persuaded of the authentic meaning of Christ's fifth word from the Cross, "I thirst"? Thérèse of Lisieux was captivated by Christ's thirsting. She marveled, for example, that Christ would have asked of the woman of Samaria, the woman at the well, the woman whose life lacked order, something to drink. "Give me a drink" (Jn 4: 7). We hear this Gospel (Jn 4: 5-42) read during Lent. The Little Flower wondered why Christ would need to beg of a foreign woman sitting at a well a drink of water. Then, like saints before her, Thérèse came to realize that the Creator of the universe was really asking for the love of this poor woman. "He thirsted," she says poignantly, "for love."[2]

Now let me address a word of encouragement to those young men who are eligible to answer the call of Christ to serve as priests. To them, I say: Look on the Cross of Christ. Listen to Jesus' word, "I thirst." If you are ready to bring souls to Christ, to lead them to life-giving waters, to slake Christ's thirst, then act on this readiness. First pray for the grace of a priestly vocation. Do not just think about being a priest. Pray for the grace to be a priest. Then talk to your pastor or a priest in your parish. Let him help you find the way to Saint Joseph's Seminary in Dunwoodie.

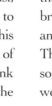

Every member of the Church should pray for vocations to the diocesan priesthood. Parish priests bear the burden of shepherding souls. Beg God to increase their number, so that when Easter comes, this year and in the future, there will be sufficient priests ready to celebrate the Supper of the Lamb. "Jesus said to them, 'Can the wedding guests mourn as long as the bridegroom is with them? The days will come when the bridegroom is taken away from them, and then they will fast...'" (Mt 9: 15). The Bridegroom is taken away. Even so, Christ has left behind men who would love his Bride with a Bridegroom's love, and so ease the "fast" that the Church must endure until he comes again.

The priest stands in the place

of Christ. Head. Shepherd. Bridegroom. It is humbling to think that Christ needs priests to satisfy his thirst for souls, but it is true. No one except the Catholic priest can say, "I absolve you." No one except the Catholic priest can say, "This is my Body. This is my Blood." Catherine of Siena, fiery mystic and compassionate sister, has this to say about Christ's thirst: "It is as if Christ said, I thirst and desire your salvation, more than the punishment of physical thirst is able to manifest. For the thirst of the body is limited, whereas the thirst of holy desire is unlimited."[3] The priest receives his sacramental consecration, his once and for all consecration, so that he can dedicate his being and his life to satisfying this unlimited "thirst of holy desire." Catherine, Doctor

of the Church, revered this priestly consecration, even when she encountered it in the person of sinful priests.[4]

Catholic priests die. The Catholic priesthood goes on for ever. It is unlimited. The Church needs many priests. Why? The Psalmist answers correctly: "My being thirsts for God, the living God. When can I go and see the face of God?" (Ps 42: 3). This thirst of holy desire, the thirst for God's love, runs on unlimitedly. And there is no way for man or woman to satisfy this thirst except through the Eucharist. Only the Catholic priest offers, consecrates, and communicates this precious gift of Christ's own self that is the Bread of Life. What a wonderful thought! The Lord who cries out, "I thirst," has already supplied for souls everywhere

I thirst.

the super-substantial wherewithal to satisfy his thirst. He gives us the gift of himself, body, blood, soul, and divinity. Young men, pray to become worthy of providing so great a gift, of satisfying so unlimited a thirst.

Notes

[1] St. Thomas Aquinas, *Lectura super Ioannem*, chap. 19, 28.

[2] "Il avait soif d'amour." From Letter 196, addressed to Sister Marie of the Sacred Heart. *Œuvres complètes* (Paris 1992), pp. 550–51. See also *Story of a Soul: The Autobiography of St. Thérèse of Lisieux*, trans. John Clarke, O.C.D. (Washington, DC: ICS Publications, 1975), pp. 100–101.

[3] Catherine of Siena, *Epistolario*, ed. Misciatelli (Siena, 1913), Letter 8, Bk. 1, p. 34; translation mine.

[4] Peter John Cameron, O.P., "Seven Last Words" St. Patrick's Cathedral, 2002: "In a mystical dialogue, God the Father reveals a stunning truth to St. Catherine of Siena: 'It is my will that the sins of the clergy should not lessen your reverence for them… Because the reverence you pay to them is not actually paid to them but to me in virtue of the blood I have entrusted to their ministry… The sacramental mystery cannot be lessened or divided by their sinfulness'" (*The Dialogue*, trans. Suzanne Noffke, O.P. [New York, 1980], no. 115).

SIXTH WORD

When Jesus had taken the wine, he said,

"IT IS FINISHED."

And bowing his head, he handed over the spirit.

Jn 19: 30

The Crucifixion

*I*t is finished" (Jn 19: 30). The first three words Jesus speaks from the Cross dispel the darkness that those who conspired to kill him tried to create. He pardons his persecutors. "Forgive them." He beatifies a common criminal who turns to him. "Today… in Paradise." He provides at once for his Mother and for the whole Church. "Behold, your son." Then a shift occurs. The next two words, the fourth and the fifth, express the exquisiteness of the suffering that Christ endures on the Cross. First, the moral suffering. "Why have you forsaken me?" Then, the physical suffering, which opens out to express the redemptive Incarnation. "I thirst." Now we come to the last two words that Christ utters from the Cross. These reveal an-

other, serene aspect of the mystery of his death, of the mystery of his obedience, of the mystery of his love. Jesus addresses his Father. He speaks the sixth word, "It is finished." The drama of Calvary becomes enveloped not in darkness, but in light. The blinding light of the Most Blessed Trinity, Father, Son, and Holy Spirit. Jesus now turns to his Father.

What is finished? The work the Father has given him. Christ himself tells us so: "I glorified you on earth by accomplishing the work that you gave me to do" (Jn 17: 4). Christ's "work" embraces the entire history of the world, backwards and forwards. The once-and-for-all sacrifice for our sins has been completed. Everything is changed. Again, Tertullian captures the truth. He refers to Christ as the *Illuminator antiquitatum*, the Illuminator of ancient times.[1] Through Christ's "work," everything becomes Christian: creation, the garden of Eden, the Fall, the Flood, the patriarchs, Moses and the prophets, the River Jordan, the new Jerusalem, the last things. Everything that has gone before and everything that lies in the future is taken up into the consummation of all things that occurs on Calvary. "It is finished." Everything that will transpire after this moment of consummation remains ordered to the Christian religion. The definitiveness of Christ's sixth word throws light on why the "Church's commitment to evangelization can never be lacking, since according to his own promise, the presence of the Lord Jesus in the power of the Holy Spirit

will never be absent from her: 'I am with you always, even until the end of the world' (Mt 28: 20)."[2] There exist no other options. No irenic compromises. No relativism. "It is finished."

How can we help but remark on the serene sovereignty of Christ's announcement. The Latin captures something of the all-embracing character of this word: "Consummatum est" (Jn 19: 30). All is consummated. The Lord Jesus refers to the course of all the centuries of the world's life. Put otherwise, the religious history of the world achieves its completion. This consummation of all things, which is realized in Christ's sacrifice of forgiveness and reconciliation, comes to the world as a gift. Nothing that men have done merits it. Quite the contrary. Instead, the gift comes from both the Father, who so loved the world that he sent his only-begotten Son, and from the incarnate Son of God, who so loved us that he offered his life in reparation for our disobedient retreat from what makes us truly happy.

This sixth word that Jesus speaks recalls the love and obedience that he enacted throughout his whole life. Death marks the final moment of Jesus' obedience. Death, however, does not bring an end to his loving. Again, it is Christ himself who says so: "Now glorify me, Father, with you, with the glory that I had with you before the world began" (Jn 17:5). The risen and exalted Savior continues to love us. Christ wants us to share in his glory. He desires that we have a share in the life of the Blessed

Trinity. Saint Paul summarizes this incredible expectation: "For you have died, and your life is hidden with Christ in God. When Christ your life appears, then you too will appear with him in glory" (Col 3: 3-4).

The consummation of all things inaugurates the new period of world history. We call it the Church. Pope Benedict XVI reminds us opportunely that "the Church as a whole and all her Pastors, like Christ, must set out to lead people out of the desert, towards the place of life, towards friendship with the Son of God, towards the One who gives us life, and life in abundance."[3]

The Pope urges us to follow Christ, *Illuminator antiquitatum*. Christ whose light enlightens the whole world.

During the Easter Vigil, the priest or deacon sings a hymn before the great candle that symbolizes Christ the Light. This hymn, the Paschal Proclamation, includes this arresting phrase: "O truly necessary sin of Adam that merited for us so great a Redeemer."[4] As she prepares to celebrate Easter, the Church reminds Christian believers that nothing surpasses their friendship with Christ. Indeed, if we were unable to enjoy this friendship, it would have been better for us never to have been born. Our own period sadly has forgotten the seriousness that our forebears in the faith expressed in their testimonies of faith. This forgetfulness places the people of our generation in great peril. They look for love in all the wrong places.

Christ's friendship is not to be taken for granted, like a common commodity that will always be available when we choose to buy it. The alternative to friendship with Christ is, in the final analysis, isolation, suffering, and disorder. Both reason and revelation dictate that we should cherish so great a gift. A worthy celebration of the Paschal mysteries demonstrates that we value Christ's friendship, and that we want this friendship to grow. C. S. Lewis says that it is characteristic of friendship to ask, "Do you care about the same truth?"[5] Do we care about "union with God through sharing in Jesus' self-gift, sharing in his body and blood"?[6] If we do, then what great delight! In the divine friendship, the shared Truth is revealed to us as a Person. And our reply to the question "Do you care?" is always the same: "I do believe, help my unbelief" (Mk 9: 24).

When the Lord speaks the sixth word from the Cross, he announces at once the end of his earthly life and the beginning of new life. New life in Christ takes on concrete realization in the Church. Again, Pope Benedict XVI speaks about a "sacramental 'mysticism.'" The sacraments of the Church do something. They are instruments of Christ's saving power. The more we are drawn into the rhythm of this divine power the more we achieve a godly perfection in our lives. "The sacramental 'mysticism,'" writes Pope Benedict, "grounded in God's condescension toward us, operates at a radically different level and lifts us to far greater heights than anything that any human mystical elevation could ever accomplish."[7]

This sacramental mysticism becomes efficaciously at work in the Church from the moment that Christ cries out, "It is finished."

New life in Christ means a life lived according to the seven sacraments of the Church. Baptism both communicates and marks the beginning of this new life. The pastors of the Church, prompted by the Holy Spirit, invite all people to change their lives, to be converted, and to be baptized.[8] They know that the "pilgrim Church is necessary for salvation."[9] The sacrament of Confirmation completes the baptismal consecration and marks the one confirmed with a special association with the bishop with whom he or she cooperates in professing the Catholic faith in the public square. Penance or reconciliation — what we call "confession" — forgives the sins committed after Baptism and, when those sins are grievous, restores the baptized Catholic to Eucharistic communion. Matrimony and Holy Orders are the sacraments of service to the communion. The Catechism gives us the teaching of Saint Thomas Aquinas: "The seven sacraments touch all the stages and all the important moments of Christian life."[10]

The sixth word from the Cross brings special consolation to us sinners. All is consummated. Everything is ready. Christ announces that the work given him by the Father is completed. "It is finished." The Gospel of John continues, "And bowing his head, he handed over the spirit." We approach the three o'clock hour. The hour of mercy. The hour when the divine mercy rushes out into the world like a torrent of crystal-clear water that cleanses the sordid and refreshes the weary. "Now glorify me, Father, with you, with the glory that

I had with you before the world began" (Jn 17: 5). Think for a moment what these words mean. Our cleansing, our renewal, our salvation, Christ considers his glory!

Notes

[1] See his *Adversus Marcionem*, Bk. IV, chap. 40 (Patrologia Latina 2:461).

[2] Congregation for the Doctrine of the Faith, 2007, "Doctrinal Note on Some Aspects of Evangelization," no. 13.

[3] Pope Benedict XVI, "Homily at the Mass for the Inauguration of the Pontificate" (24 April 2005): *Acta Apostolicae Sedes* 97 (2005): 710.

[4] Roman Liturgy, Easter Proclamation (*Exsultet*).

[5] C. S. Lewis, *The Four Loves* (London: Collins/Fontana Books, 1965), p. 62.

[6] Pope Benedict XVI, *Deus caritas est*, no. 13.

[7] *Deus caritas est*, no. 14.

[8] See Encyclical Letter of John Paul II, *Redemptoris missio* (7 December 1990), no. 47, as cited in the 2007 "Doctrinal Note on Some Aspects of Evangelization" by the Congregation for the Doctrine of the Faith, no. 1.

[9] Second Vatican Council, Dogmatic Constitution *Lumen gentium*, no. 14.

[10] As summarized in the *Catechism of the Catholic Church*, par. 1210.

 EVENTH WORD

It was now about noon and darkness came over the whole land until three in the afternoon because of an eclipse of the sun. Then the veil of the temple was torn down the middle. Jesus cried out in a loud voice,

"FATHER, INTO YOUR HANDS I COMMEND MY SPIRIT";

and when he had said this he breathed his last.

Lk 23: 44-46

The Face of the Crucified Jesus

ather, into your hands I commend my spirit" (Lk 23: 46). All who accept the Gospel of Christ are bound to pray these words. Each must repeat daily this seventh of Christ's words from the Cross. We especially must make this seventh word our own. Why? Like marriage, death remains an inevitable circumstance of life. And the established rule still holds good: we die as we live.

The Catholic believer does not wait for the moment of death to commend for the first time himself or herself to the heavenly Father. The Catholic believer repeats Christ's seventh word in every circumstance of life. There is not a moment in our daily lives that does not require from us an act of submission to God's will.

This general rule of Catholic living does not suppress our human freedom. On the contrary, self-committal to God perfects us, opens us out, rejoices our souls. Rebelliousness destroys, closes in, and saddens our being. Personal surrender to God sanctifies those who surrender only when their surrender is joined to the self-gift of God's Son. In other words, we cannot do it on our own. The Savior of the human race is just that. He alone conducts a sin-ridden world to the Love that never ends. Those who commend themselves to God in union with Jesus commit themselves to sharing his acts of filial love and obedience. When they do this, they will recall what today remains a much-forgotten condition of Christian discipleship, of Catholic living, of life in the Church. It is a condition that Christ himself places upon his disciples: "Amen, I say to you, unless you turn and become like children, you will not enter the kingdom of heaven" (Mt 18: 3).

Children need to be fed. In the plan of God, the Eucharist each day supplies nourishment for God's children. We should never forget that

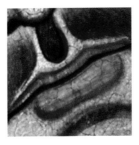

Christ instituted the Eucharist shortly before his death: "I received"—it is Saint Paul who speaks—"from the Lord what I handed on to you, namely, that the Lord Jesus, on the night in which he was betrayed took bread, and, after he had given thanks…" (1 Cor 11: 23-24a). From that moment on, the Eucharist announces Christ's Passion and death. "Christ has died." One reason for the bond between the Eucharist and the Passion is simple to understand: if Christ had not died for our sins, no human person could hope to achieve the virtues that the Eucharist causes to flourish in our lives. We would still remain in our original rebelliousness: scattered, unloved, unloving. In the most Blessed Sacrament, God bestows gifts of unity and of charity and of communion that only he can create. The communion of persons created in the Eucharist surpasses anything that the whole human race, not to mention any individual, could ever hope to achieve unaided. This communion of persons is not one option among many for living. It presents the only option. Truth to tell, no alternative in life exists other than the self-committal that Christ expresses in his last word from the Cross. "Father, into your hands I commend my spirit" (Lk 23: 46).

God never works in us against our deliberate wills. The Church requires that we ready ourselves to celebrate the Eucharist, to receive Holy Communion, in order to join the communion of beatitude. We must confess our sins, when necessary, and in any case renew our sorrow for past sins, so that the virtues of Christ's Passion can take new and deep root in our heart. Without this renewal of the whole person, it is impossible to know and to experience the grace for which we must always give Eucharistic thanks. Christ prayed that we would receive this grace: "Father, they are your gift to me. I wish that where I am they also may be with me, that they may see my glory that you gave me, because you loved me before the foundation of the world" (Jn 17: 24).

Holy Communion strengthens the friendship that Christ desires to develop with each of us. Of course, the Eucharist takes the form of a meal, but this Blessed Sacrament is not ultimately about eating and drinking. "By the reality of his body and blood," Saint Thomas Aquinas clarifies for us, "Christ joins us to himself in this sacrament."[1] The Eucharist is about communion. Aquinas goes on therefore to explain that it is proper to friendship that friends live with one another (*convivere amicis*). We can never take for granted the fact that Christ chooses to remain friends with us. We should never forget his words: "I have called you friends" (Jn 15: 15). We should know that, in the end, Christ is our best friend. The Best Friend. Whereas it is a majestic mystery that Jesus Christ remains present with us in the tabernacles of the world, greater still is the truth that Christ wants to draw us intimately close to himself, to transform us into his Body. This loving communion with the persons of the Blessed Trinity remains the destiny to which each creature made in the divine image is called. Again, Christ's words to his disciples announce our destiny: "I wish that where I am they also may be with me, that they may see my glory that you gave me, because you loved me before the foundation of the world" (Jn 17: 24). *Convivere amicis*. To live with one's friends.

"Father, into your hands I commend my spirit." The Eucharist renews daily our self-committal, our submission, our obedience to God. At each celebration of the Mass, we unite ourselves with Christ's own sacrifice. Christ's choice to give himself over on Calvary, to give himself over in the Eucharist, separates him from the ordinary martyrs. They accepted

what befell them. Christ on the other hand chose with his human will the death that consummates his self-giving, "with his human will, not simply as accepting a fact but as producing an effect."[2] He chose it because of his free obedience to the Father. "I lay down my life in order to take it up again. No one takes it from me, but I lay it down on my own"(Jn 10: 17-18). He chose it because of his love for us. "Though he was harshly treated, he submitted and opened not his mouth" (Is 53: 7). He chose it as the cause of our redemption. "For you had gone astray like sheep, but you have now returned to the shepherd and guardian of your souls" (1 Pt 2: 25).

The Eucharist accompanies us along the course of our life. When death comes, the priest still brings the Eucharist. The Church calls this Holy Communion Viaticum, food for the journey. Those who have commended themselves to God throughout a lifetime fear not making the final commendation. They show no hesitation at that moment when, for the last time, they must repeat Christ's seventh word from the Cross: "Father, into your hands."

The Church provides a special sacrament of healing for the sick and dying. Holy Anointing forms a central part of the "sacramental 'mysticism'" that Pope Benedict XVI has recommended to both our meditation and our practice. The drama of the Last Words unfolds in a world where Adam's sin affects every member of the human race: "Through one person," Saint Paul writes with reference to Adam, "sin entered the world, and through sin, death, and thus death came to all, inasmuch as all sinned" (Rom 5: 12). Each sacrament of the Christian life provides its own specific remedies for the effects of Adam's sin. Holy Anointing received at the hands of the priest or bishop brings the power of Christ's sacrifice to bear on the last enemy that no human being escapes. As Saint Paul says expressly: "The last enemy to be destroyed is death, for 'he subjected everything under his feet'" (1 Cor 15: 26-27).

Holy Anointing disposes every man and woman to make their own the prayer that Christ prays from the Cross, "Father, into your hands I commend my spirit." And should this moment arrive when we are no longer conscious, the Church speaks the prayer for us. Something similar occurs at Baptism, when parents and godparents speak for their child and godchild the baptismal promises. The prayer of the Church and the anointing with oil urges the dying Catholic to make his or her own Christ's complete subjection to the Father. In other words, at the end we find ourselves placed, inevitably, as it were, in the proper ordering to God. "'Father, into your hands I commend my spirit,' and when he had said this he breathed his last."

No one escapes death. The only question to answer is whether I will die religiously or not. Whether I will die submitting myself to God or turning away from him. Whether I will die bathed in the light of the Paschal mystery that Christ consummates at this hour or die excluded from him in the darkness. Before Christ's sac-rificial death on the Cross, the only option for the human race was darkness. Darkness for the just, darkness for the wicked. The just awaited the moment of Christ's death, for the power of Christ's sacrifice worked backward and forward. Christ dies in his humanity, but the Incarnation is not dissolved. "He descended to the dead," we profess in the Apostles' Creed. This means that Christ descends to the dark place where the Old Testament saints such as Adam and Eve, Abel, Abraham, Moses, King David, and the prophets, awaited his glorious arrival. And Christ led them out, victoriously.

Christ still leads victoriously. His royal banners carry on. He leads those who hear his words and follow them. It is three o'clock. Christ has died. We take our inspiration from one of the Catholic epistles, the Letter of James: "Be doers of the word and not hearers only, deluding yourselves. For if anyone is a hearer of the word and not a doer, he is like a man who looks at his own face in a mirror. He sees himself, then goes off and promptly forgets what he looked like. But the one who peers into the perfect law of freedom and perseveres, and is not a hearer who forgets but a doer who acts, such a one shall be blessed in what he does" (Ja 1: 22-25). "O beloved Spouse of souls, kiss us at this hour from thy Cross." For ever and ever. Amen.

---

1 St. Thomas Aquinas, *Summa theologiae* III, q. 75, art. 1. Adapted from the Blackfriars edition (1965): "He [Christ] joins us to himself in this sacrament in the reality of his body and blood."

2 Cardinal Cajetan makes this point, and uses these texts in his third *Jentaculum* (Poznan, 1524). See Charles Journet, *L'Eglise du Verbe incarné*, Bk. 1, chap. 3. A one-volume abridged version exists in English: *Theology of the Church* (San Francisco: Ignatius Press, 2004).

CONCLUSION

The Women at the Tomb

In 1872, Good Friday fell on March 29. At the Church of Saint Vincent Ferrer on Lexington Avenue, New Yorkers welcomed a visiting preacher from Ireland by the name of Father Thomas Burke. He delivered a sermon entitled "Christ on Calvary," basing his reflections on the text "Come, all you who pass by the  way, look and see, Whether there is any suffering like my suffering" (Lam 1: 12). He brought his nineteenth-century sermon to a close with these words: "It is well to rejoice and be here; it is well to come and contemplate the blessings which that blessed, gracious Lord has conferred on us. It is, also, well to consider what He paid and how much it cost Him. And if we consider this, then with Mary, the mother, and Mary, the Magdalen, and John, the Evangelist and friend—then will our hearts be afflicted. For the soul that is not afflicted on this day, shall be wiped out from the pages of the Book of Life."[1] The rhetoric has changed, but not the message.

The Book of Life. What is it? According to the tradition, the Book of Life contains the names of the elect. Catholic faith always avoids extreme positions. No one knows the contents of the Book of Life. Nothing prohibits everyone's name from being found therein. Neither is there an assurance that everyone's name is written in the Book of Life.[2] Saints throughout the ages have cautioned against fretting or scrupulous preoccupation about the Book's contents. Pope Benedict

XVI develops this caution to encourage us to think about Final Judgment as a moment of justice and grace. "The incarnation of God in Christ," says the Pope, "has so closely linked the two together — judgment and grace — that justice is firmly established: we all work out our salvation 'with fear and trembling' (Phil 2: 12)."[3]

How do we work out our salvation with

fear and trembling, while at the same time maintaining the most firm hope in the power of Christ's sacrifice to save us. The practical, Catholic answer is simple and clear: practice the sacraments. Discover why Pope Benedict has coined the expression "sacramental 'mysticism.'"[4] There is no replacement for the sacraments that Christ instituted for our salvation. In each of them, we meet Christ.

Each sacrament affords Catholics a moment of affliction for their sins and creates a moment of consolation for their redemption.

It remains a safe generalization that considerable confusion still exists among Catholics about the importance of the sacraments, the reception of the sacraments, the fruitfulness of the sacraments. This is not the place to address the causes of the confusion. But we can propose a solution for the confusion. The Catholic people must ponder exhaustively the implications of Christ's words: "It is finished." Everything that is needed for us to acquire the redemption won by Christ on the Cross exists. What remains for us, for the Church, for the Church's pastors, is to ensure that all human persons discover the "sacramental 'mysticism'" that makes us and keeps us friends of God.

One sign that meditation on the events of Good Friday has brought a salutary affliction to our souls is our reception of the sacrament of penance. It is impossible to overestimate the importance of the confessional, the place of reconciliation. Without sacramental reconciliation administered by a priest, we lose our capacity to stand transparent before the Lord. Instead we imitate what is recorded about our first parents once the effect of their sin became apparent. We hide. We hide from the Lord, who continues nonetheless to announce that the work of our redemption has been completed. "It is finished." Good Friday confirms that no reason exists to hide from "the One who gives us life, and life in abundance."[5]

When we confess our sins, the Church requires in ordinary circumstances a particular confession of sins. That is, she asks that we entrust ourselves with honesty and courage to the divine mercy that forgives, as Saint Jerome reminds us, "for if the sick person is too ashamed to show his wound to the doctor, the doctor cannot heal what he does not know."[6] Pope John Paul II explains that "confession in a way forces sin out of the secret of the heart and thus out of the area of pure individuality."[7] To be sure, this feature of sacramental reconciliation causes considerable difficulty for not a few souls. Many of us would have hoped for an easier form of forgiveness, one that dispenses with the need to examine our lives as well as our consciences. So it is important to see that God provides something much better for us sinners than the chance to hide behind our own pride and excuses. A few acts of confidence and love are worth more than a thousand skirtings and maybes. There is no such thing as counterfeit contrition.

Christ is the truly religious man, the just one, who has restored an order that is written into the very being of creation. It is an order that requires submission to the God who made heaven and earth. It is an order that recognizes human freedom as a mark of the divine, even as it exhorts free men and women that they "continually offer God a sacrifice of praise" (Heb 13: 15). It is an order where love counts more than anything else. It is an order that does not count the cost of discipleship. Recall what Christ said when the mother of the sons of Zebedee sought preference for her sons. Can they drink of my cup? Be baptized with my baptism? (See Mt 20: 22, 23.) Saint Augustine asked us to overlook the impudence of this dear woman. The maternal

instinct, he said, knows no patience. It is difficult not to think that Saint Augustine's theological explanation was developed out of his own personal experience. His own mother, Saint Monica, never gave up on him. She exhausted the divine patience.

There is something comforting in the maternal solicitude that holy women show toward their children. Recently I came across a striking example of rectified maternal loving illustrated in a stained-glass window of a chapel in the west of France. The wayside chapel near the city of Angers marks the place where at the end of the eighteenth century more than two thousand Catholic believers were peremptorily executed by the revolutionary forces in France that were the first to give modern Europe a sampling of fanatical genocide. These holy men and women collectively are revered as martyrs, having died at the hands of the French Revolutionaries.

These everyday French martyrs include the priest Blessed Noël Pinot (d. 1794), who was arrested while preparing to celebrate a clandestine Mass for his parishioners, and shortly thereafter guillotined for what the ideological fanatics called "fanaticism." To expose to ridicule his priestly consecration, the executioners led him to the guillotine dressed in his priestly vestments. As Father Pinot mounted the platform, he began the prayers that, at that time, were prescribed for the beginning of Mass. "Introibo ad altare Dei." They are the words of the Psalmist, "I will go unto the altar of God, to God, my joy, my delight" (see Ps 43: 4).

In addition to Noël Pinot, there are ninety-nine other persons recognized as Blessed. These are the ones for whom some records remained. These ninety-nine were beatified by Pope John Paul II in 1984.[8] Of these ninety-nine persons brutally executed by guillotine or shooting, eighty were laywomen – laywomen from every station and walk of life. They offer a startling witness to the power of divine grace transforming human life in the most arduous circumstances. One of these women, a mother, stands out. She is Blessed Perrine-Charlotte Phelippeaux, in marriage Sailland d'Epinatz, a fifty-four-year-old mother, who was condemned to death for practicing the Catholic faith—for refusing to abandon its sacramental mysticism. Condemned with her were her three daughters, Madeleine, twenty-four, Jeanne, twenty-five, and Perrine, twenty-six.

Blessed Perrine-Charlotte is depicted in the stained-glass window giving the last gold coins in her possession to the hapless revolutionary who was about to execute her and her children. What was this mother's request? That the executioner shoot her  daughters first so that they would not have to endure the horror of seeing their mother killed. Perrine-Charlotte of course wanted to encourage these young demoiselles until their end came. Whereas Judas sold Christ for pieces of silver, Blessed Perrine-Charlotte bought mercy with her last pieces of gold. Gold, moreover, given to the man who would kill her and her maiden daughters. Can one imagine a more illuminating reflection of Christ's serene self-donation? His Passover? A more illustrative image of his compassionate love for others?

When you want to understand what it means that, by his death on the Cross, Christ establishes a new order of love, when you want to recall how much Catholics have cherished the sacramental mysticism that channels his love, when you want to measure the effect that Christ's death has had on the world, think first not of this preacher's words. Think of Blessed Noël Pinot, martyred priest of the Mass and of the sacraments. Think especially of Blessed Perrine-Charlotte. A Christian woman and mother. A witness to love both maternal and compassionate, to love serenely expressed. Like Christ on the cross. Think of her young daughters in their twenties, Blesseds Perrine, Jeanne, and Madeleine Sailland d'Epinatz. Think of all who have died rather than deny the new law of love. Think of all those who have died for professing the Creed and celebrating the sacraments. Most recently in 2008, Paulos Faraj Rahho, the assassinated archbishop of Mosul in Iraq. Think of all who have given their lives so that the saving Gospel of Jesus Christ can reach the ends of the world.

The witness of the woman martyrs of the French Revolution, especially Blessed Perrine-Charlotte, instructs us. She displayed dramatically what two centuries later Pope John Paul II would call the "feminine genius." Like all holy women, Blessed Perrine-Charlotte points us to the Blessed Virgin Mary. *Ad Jesum per Mariam*. To Jesus through Mary. To learn well the divine truths that Jesus speaks to us from the Cross, join the company of the Virgin Mother of God, Mary Immaculate, and especially in this year, which marks the 150th anniversary of her appearance in Lourdes. Let Mary open your hearts to hear whatever Jesus would tell you to do. Then, as Mary herself instructs us, "'Do whatever he tells you'" (Jn 2: 5).

Notes

[1] *Lectures and Sermons By The Very Rev. T. N. Burke, O.P.* (New York: P. M. Haverty, 1872), pp. 137–59, at 159.

[2] See Saint Thomas Aquinas, *Summa theologiae* I, q. 24, esp. art. 3.

[3] Encyclical Letter (2007) of Pope Benedict XVI, *Spe salvi*, no. 47.

[4] Pope Benedict XVI has long meditated on the importance that the Church and her Doctors, men and women, have attached to the pierced side of Christ. In fact, one of his first books translated into English is entitled *Behold the Pierced One*. See Joseph Cardinal Ratzinger, *Behold the Pierced One*, trans. Graham Harrison (San Francisco: Ignatius Press, 1986).

[5] Pope Benedict XVI, "Homily at the Mass for the Inauguration of the Pontificate" (24 April 2005): *Acta Apostolicae Sedes* 97 (2005): 710.

[6] St. Jerome, *Commentarii in Ecclesiasten* 10, 11 (Patrologiae Latina 23:1096).

[7] Post-Synodal Exhortation of Pope John Paul II, *Reconciliatio et Poenitentia* (1984), no. 31.

[8] See the Vatican website, "List of Blesseds and Saints proclaimed during the Pontificate of John Paul II," 1984: "The Martyrs of Angers during French Revolution: Fr. William Repin and 98 Companions."

Printed in February 2009
by Transcontinental, Canada

www.magnificat.com